Sara Swan Miller

Woodpeckers, Toucans, and Their Kin

Franklin Watts - A Division of Scholastic Inc.
New York • Toronto • London • Auckland • Sydney
Mexico City • New Delhi • Hong Kong
Danbury, Connecticut

Photographs © 2002: Corbis Images/Maurizio Lanini: 37; Dembinsky Photo Assoc.: 17 (Sharon Cummings), 13 (Dan Dempster), 35 (Alan G. Nelson), cover (Jim Roetzel), 5 top left (Dick Scott), 6 (George Stewart); Minden Pictures: 27 (Claus Meyer), 1 (Konrad Wothe); NFI Transvaal Museum: 33 (A. Goetz/FitzPatrick Bird Communication Library); Photo Researchers, NY: 39 (Stephen Dalton), 31 (Nigel Dennis), 5 bottom right (Francois Gohier), 5 top right, 29 (Jacana), 23 (Bud Lehnhausen), 5 bottom left (Maslowski), 42 (William H. Mullins), 19, 21 (Gregory K. Scott), 41 (Roger Wilmshurst); VIREO/Academy of Natural Sciences of Philadelphia: 25 (J. Dunning); Visuals Unlimited: 7 (Bill Beatty), 15 (Gerald & Buff Corsi), 43 (Rob & Ann Simpson)

Illustrations by Pedro Julio Gonzalez and Steve Savage.

The photo on the cover shows a downy woodpecker pecking on a branch. The photo on the title page shows a toco toucan in a tree.

Library of Congress Cataloging-in-Publication Data

Miller, Sara Swan.
    Woodpeckers, toucans, and their kin / Sara Swan Miller.
    p. cm. – (Animals in order)
    Summary: Introduces the different animals in the piciform order, their similarities and differences, environments in which they live, and how to observe them.
    Includes bibliographical references and index.
    ISBN 0-531-12243-3 (lib. bdg.)   0-531-16661-9 (pbk.)
    1. Piciformes—Juvenile literature. [1. Woodpeckers. 2. Toucans.] I. Title. II. Series.
QL696.P5 M56 2003
598.7'2—dc21   2002001732

Contents

Meet the Piciformes: From Woodpeckers to Toucans

Have you ever watched a big pileated woodpecker loudly drilling a huge hole in a tree? Have you ever seen a yellow-bellied sapsucker busily pecking a row of little holes in tree bark? You may have guessed that these birds were related.

If you did, you were right! Both woodpeckers and sapsuckers are in the same group, or order, of animals. The name of this order is *piciformes* (pie-see-FORM-eez), which means "woodpecker-like." Woodpeckers "pick" at trees with their chisel-shaped bills.

You might be surprised to know that there are many other birds in this order that, at first glance, don't seem much like woodpeckers. Toucans, for instance, have huge, broad bills that are half as long as the rest of their bodies. Little barbets have stubby bills and feed mostly on fruits. Jacamars fly about, snatching insects out of the air with their long, slender bills. How can they all be related to woodpeckers?

On the next page are four piciformes. Can you guess what these very different-looking birds all have in common?

Pileated woodpecker

Toco toucan

Northern flicker

Rufous-tailed jacamar

Traits of the Piciformes

If you could get a good look at these birds' feet, you might notice something special about them. Two toes point forward, and two point backward. The piciformes are one of the few groups of birds that have these *zygodactyl* (zye-go-DAK-till) *feet*. Most piciformes have four toes, although two species have only three. The piciformes' feet help them brace themselves as they climb up tree trunks.

Piciformes have other things in common. They all nest in holes—usually tree holes—and most of them hollow out their own. All the birds in this order lay white eggs.

There are a few other similarities. Most piciformes don't have down feathers under their outer feathers. Most of them have thick skulls and long tongues, which are often barbed or sticky. Many of them have stiff tail feathers, which give them support as they climb up trees.

Scientists have found other things these birds have in common. They can tell that piciformes have unusual head bones and muscles.

Most piciformes have two toes that point forward and two toes that point backward.

6

Scientists also look at how their feathers grow and compare them to other birds' feather patterns.

But what explains the variety of bills, shapes, and habits of these birds? Scientists believe that they had a common ancestor, which may have looked a lot like the little barbets of today. Over millions of years they adapted in ways that suited their different lifestyles. This is known as *divergent evolution*. Species in an order diverge as they adapt to different needs.

There are about 370 different species of piciformes living in many different habitats around the world. Different species can be found in woodlands, rain forests, savannahs, deserts, and even cities and suburbs.

Many piciformes have long, sticky tongues.

The Order of Living Things

A tiger has more in common with a house cat than with a daisy. A true bug is more like a butterfly than a jellyfish. Scientists arrange living things into groups based on how they look and how they act. A tiger and a house cat belong to the same group, but a daisy belongs to a different group.

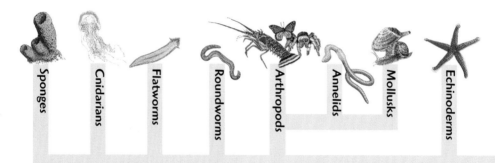

Sponges | Cnidarians | Flatworms | Roundworms | Arthropods | Annelids | Mollusks | Echinoderms

Animals

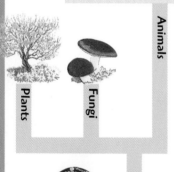

Plants | Fungi

Monerans | Protists

All living things can be placed in one of five groups called *kingdoms*: the plant kingdom, the animal kingdom, the fungus kingdom, the moneran kingdom, or the protist kingdom. You can probably name many of the creatures in the plant and animal kingdoms. The fungus kingdom includes mushrooms, yeasts, and molds. The moneran and protist kingdoms contain thousands of living things that are too small to see without a microscope.

8

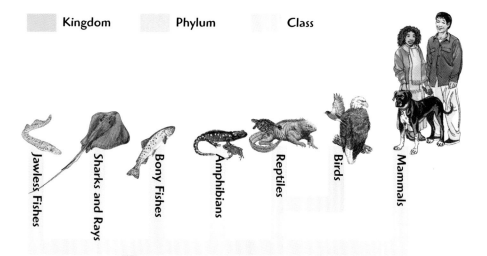

Kingdom Phylum Class

Jawless Fishes

Sharks and Rays

Bony Fishes

Amphibians

Reptiles

Birds

Mammals

Chordates

Because there are millions and millions of living things on Earth, some of the members of one kingdom may not seem all that similar. The animal kingdom includes creatures as different as tarantulas and trout, jellyfish and jaguars, salamanders and sparrows, elephants and earthworms.

To show that an elephant is more like a jaguar than an earthworm, scientists further separate the creatures in each kingdom into more specific groups. The animal kingdom can be divided into nine *phyla*. Humans belong to the chordate phylum. All chordates have a backbone.

Each phylum can be subdivided into many *classes*. Humans, mice, and elephants all belong to the mammal class. Each class can be further divided into *orders*; orders into *families*, families into *genera*, and genera into *species*. All the members of a species are very similar.

How Piciformes Fit In

You can probably guess that piciformes belong to the animal kingdom. They have much more in common with spiders and snakes than they do with maple trees and morning glories.

Piciformes belong to the chordate phylum. Almost all chordates have backbones and skeletons. Can you think of other chordates? Examples include elephants, mice, snakes, frogs, fish, and whales.

The chordate phylum can be divided into a number of classes. All birds belong to the same class. There are about thirty different orders of birds. Piciformes make up one of these orders.

The piciformes can be divided into six different families and a number of different genera. The genera can be broken down into hundreds of species that live on all the continents except Australia and Antarctica. In this book, you will learn more about fifteen different species of piciformes.

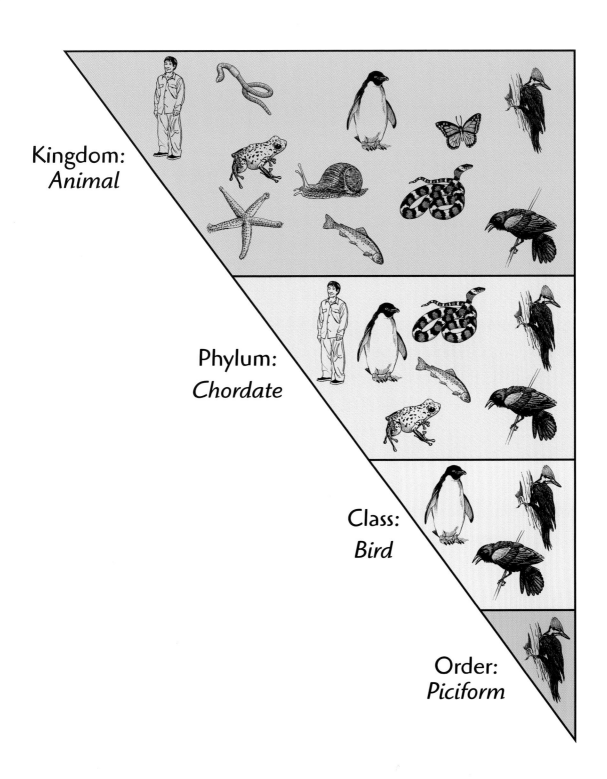

Kingdom:
Animal

Phylum:
Chordate

Class:
Bird

Order:
Piciform

Woodpeckers

FAMILY: Picidae
COMMON EXAMPLE: Pileated woodpecker
GENUS AND SPECIES: *Dryocopus pileatus*
SIZE: 16 1/2 inches (42 cm)

Is that a pterodactyl flying through the woods? A huge, primitive-looking pileated woodpecker soars to a tree and lands with a thump on the trunk. "Kik-kik-kikkik-kik-kik!" he calls. He sounds like Woody Woodpecker laughing! Now he starts drumming loudly on the trunk with his chisel-like beak. What is he doing? Searching for insects under the bark? Digging a nest hole? Not this time. It's mating season, and he is drumming to attract his mate.

A pair of male and female pileated woodpeckers stay near each other all year round and call back and forth to keep in contact. When spring comes, they get even noisier. Finally, the female lets the male know she's ready to mate. She perches across a branch and calls out "Awoick-awoick!"

After they mate, both birds set to work hollowing out a nest hole in an old, rotting tree. They take turns working, until they have created a large, rectangular hole about 3 1/2 inches (69 cm) from top to bottom.

Pileated woodpeckers are excellent parents. They take turns sitting on the eggs while the other one stays nearby. Once the eggs hatch, the parents take turns feeding the chicks for as long as four weeks. Even after the *fledglings* leave the nest, they beg their parents for food. Three months later, the parents are still willing to share food with their young. Most other young birds would be on their own long before that!

Woodpeckers

FAMILY: Picidae
COMMON EXAMPLE: Acorn woodpecker
GENUS AND SPECIES: *Melanerpes formicivorus*
SIZE: 9 inches (23 cm)

Winter is on the way, and an acorn woodpecker is busy storing food. It flies from tree to tree, plucking acorns one at a time. With an acorn in its bill, it flies to its storage tree and sticks the acorn into a hole it has drilled. Then off it flies in search of another acorn.

Acorn woodpeckers choose trees with thick, dry bark to use as storage trees. They drill as many as sixty thousand holes in a single tree, although not all of them get filled with acorns. Acorn woodpeckers are not about to share their acorns with anyone else. Any intruders will be quickly driven away.

You may have guessed that acorns are an acorn woodpecker's favorite winter food. But in the warmer months, it finds plenty of other things to eat. Tree sap is another favorite. Acorn woodpeckers get together in groups to sip sap from holes they have drilled over the years in good, sap-yielding trees. At other times, they sit on the tops of trees and snap up insects that are flying by. Sometimes they feed on flower nectar or fruit. They will even eat birds' eggs and small lizards if they come across them.

You will hardly ever see acorn woodpeckers on the ground. They feel much safer in the trees. But every so often, one will fly down to

retrieve a fallen acorn or to pick up pieces of grit that it eats to help digest its food.

Acorn woodpeckers live in oak forests in the western United States, where there are plenty of acorns for the taking. Although these woodpeckers are still abundant, they may become rare as people keep destroying oak forests for firewood and timber.

Flickers

FAMILY: Picidae
COMMON EXAMPLE: Northern flicker
GENUS AND SPECIES: *Colaptes auratus*
SIZE: 12 1/2 inches (32 cm)

What is that flicker doing bobbing around on the ground? Aren't woodpeckers supposed to live in trees? Not this one. The flicker is searching for its favorite food—ants. Flickers eat more ants than any other North American bird does. They will also eat beetles, termites, and caterpillars. In the fall, they sometimes eat fruits and berries, or even an occasional seed or nut. Mostly, though, they are ant eaters.

If you spot a pair of flickers one spring, you can be fairly certain that you will see them again year after year. Flickers pair for life, and after they migrate south for the winter, they always return to the same area to mate and raise their young. They often return to the same tree. Flickers have weak bills compared to other woodpeckers. Since they aren't strong drillers, they need to find rotting trees with soft wood to make their nests in. Once a pair of flickers has discovered a good tree, the two will use it again and again.

Northern flickers are one of the few woodpeckers that migrate. When spring comes, the males come back first. You may hear them yelling, "Wick-wick-wick-wick!" or drumming on a tree trunk. This is their way of announcing their presence and driving away other males.

When a female arrives, she is immediately attracted to her noisy mate. The two *court* each other by bobbing up and down and calling, "Woikawoikawoika." Once they're done courting, both birds set to work digging out a nest hole, although the male does most of the work. He helps sit on the eggs too. In fact, he takes over the job completely at night, while the female roosts in another hole nearby.

Woodpeckers

FAMILY: Picidae
COMMON EXAMPLE: Downy woodpecker
GENUS AND SPECIES: *Picoides pubescens*
SIZE: 6 inches (15 cm)

Tap! Tap! Tap! A male downy woodpecker is busily hunting for insects in the treetops. He digs long tunnels into the bark of trees with his chisel-like bill. Then he zips out his long, sticky tongue and quickly catches the beetles, ants, and termites hiding inside.

Like many other woodpeckers, downies are well suited to drilling into trees to snag insects. Their head bones act as a kind of helmet to protect their brains from being hurt by all the drumming they do. Their tongues are very long and have sharp barbs that latch onto insects inside the tunnels they have drilled. They also have big *salivary glands* that produce large amounts of very sticky saliva that traps their prey.

Woodpeckers have slender tongues, longer than any other bird's, which they can stick deep into trees. But where do they store their tongues? Amazingly, a woodpecker's tongue wraps around the top of its skull when the woodpecker isn't feeding. The tongue is anchored inside the right nostril, then goes up between the eyes, over the top of the skull, down the back of the skull, and finally through the beak.

Spring is mating time for downy woodpeckers. The males and females call to each other with a quiet "pic" and a loud rattling

noise. The female chooses the nest site. It's the male's job to dig out the nest. It takes less than two weeks for the eggs to hatch. Then both parents feed the hungry hatchlings with fresh insects. Even after they have begun to fly, the young stay with their parents for several weeks, begging for food.

Sapsuckers

FAMILY: Picidae
COMMON EXAMPLE: Yellow-bellied sapsucker
GENUS AND SPECIES: *Sphyrapicus varius*
SIZE: 8 1/2 inches (22 cm)

Most woodpeckers feed on insects, but yellow-bellied sapsuckers eat sap too. They drill tiny holes in neatly spaced rows into tree bark to make the sap flow. Then they use their brushlike tongues to wipe up the sap that oozes out. Sapsuckers return to the same trees again and again to suck up sap from the wells they have created. Once young sapsuckers can fly, their parents teach them how to drill for sap too.

Sapsuckers don't live entirely on sap, though. They also eat the insects that get stuck in the sticky sap, especially ants. In the fall, they enjoy berries and fruits.

Without meaning to, sapsuckers do other animals a favor when they drill their sap wells. Other woodpeckers, warblers, and even hummingbirds visit the sapsuckers' wells. Chipmunks and squirrels enjoy the sweet sap too.

Yellow-bellied sapsuckers are widespread in North America, but you may not notice them. They are the quietest of all woodpeckers, even at mating time. During mating season, the males and females call to each other with little squeaks and whines. The male also drums as other woodpeckers do, but quietly. If you listen hard, you can learn to recognize a yellow-bellied sapsucker's drumming. It starts

fast, then quickly slows down. Sapsuckers are well camouflaged and very shy. When a sapsucker spots someone coming through the woods, it will quietly hitch itself around to the other side of the tree it's clinging to. You need to be very quiet and alert if you want to spot a sapsucker.

Jacamars

FAMILY: Galbulidae
COMMON EXAMPLE: Rufous-tailed jacamar
GENUS AND SPECIES: *Galbula ruficauda*
SIZE: 8 inches (20 cm)

A rufous-tailed jacamar sits upright on a branch over a river with its long, slender bill tilted in the air. It moves its head left, right, up, and down, peering for insects with its glittering eyes. Suddenly, it spots a butterfly floating by. It zips from its perch on whirring wings and grabs the butterfly in its bill. Quickly, the jacamar flies back to its perch with its struggling prey and bangs it over and over on the branch. Soon the butterfly's wings break off and fall to the ground, and the jacamar gobbles up its juicy meal.

You might think that a jacamar's long, thin bill wouldn't be a very good tool for catching flying insects, but it actually works quite well. When a jacamar grabs a butterfly or a dragonfly, its long bill can reach over the wings and grasp the body. If its bill were shorter, the jacamar might find itself with nothing but a billful of dry wing. Its long bill can also hold an insect's flailing wings away from the jacamar's head while it beats its prey against a branch. That long bill is a good tool for holding stinging wasps away from a jacamar's face too.

A jacamar's bill isn't quite as good for digging a nest hole, though. Tree trunks are too hard, so jacamars usually dig their holes in the banks of streams. Together, a male and female dig a tunnel about

22

20 inches (50 cm) long. The female lays her eggs on the bare ground inside. Both parents bring insects to the hatchlings. While they wait for the next meal, the young practice singing the complicated songs of their parents.

Puffbirds

FAMILY: Bucconidae
COMMON EXAMPLE: White-fronted nunbird
GENUS AND SPECIES: *Monasa morphoeus*
SIZE: 11 1/2 inches (29 cm)

A white-fronted nunbird is one of more than thirty species of puffbirds that live in different parts of South America. Unlike most puffbirds, which are fat birds with short wings and puffy feathers, the nunbird is slim and has longer, stronger wings. Like other puffbirds, it has bristles around its beak that help it catch the insects it eats.

When it's on the hunt for insects, a nunbird sits quietly among the leaves on a tree, peering all around. Suddenly, it swoops from its perch, snatches a passing insect, and flies quickly back to its perch to gobble up its meal. A nunbird will also pick off insects creeping on the leaves or down on the ground. Sometimes, nunbirds follow after bands of monkeys to eat the insects they stir up. Nunbirds sometimes eat small lizards and other small invertebrates.

When they're not hunting, white-fronted nunbirds are incredibly noisy. They have all kinds of calls, from a wooden rattle to soft, deep notes. A flock of them will all sit together on a branch, lift up their heads, and shout out their ringing calls. This can go on for twenty minutes at a time!

When it's time to lay eggs, a male and female dig a tunnel about 20 inches (50 cm) long in the ground and line it with dead leaves.

They camouflage the entrance with a collar of leaves and sticks. The young birds who were born the year before help to feed the hatchlings. Born blind and naked, the little birds have to stumble all the way up the long tunnel to get a mouthful of crushed insects. Finally, about thirty days after they are born, they come out and fly off to find their own food.

Toucans

FAMILY: Ramphastidae
COMMON EXAMPLE: Toco toucan
GENUS AND SPECIES: *Ramphastos toco*
SIZE: 24 inches (60 cm)

What an enormous bill! How can a toco toucan fly with that giant thing on its face? A toucan's bill is actually not as heavy as it looks. The outside is hard and horny, but the inside is hollow. It is criss-crossed with thin, bony rods that support it. Yet even with the bony rods for support, a toucan's bill is fragile and can break easily.

A toucan's bill is a wonderful tool. The big toucan perches on a thick branch and reaches far out to pluck a fruit or berry from the tip of a small twig that is too fragile to support the toucan's weight. It seizes a fruit with the tip of its bill and throws it into the back of its throat. Its long, bristly tongue catches the fruit, and down it goes.

A toucan has other uses for its huge, gaudy bill. When it pounces on a nest full of baby birds, the huge bill startles the parents so badly that they don't think of fighting back. The toucan can just reach in, pluck out a helpless baby bird, and gulp it down. A toucan uses its bill to snap up insects, lizards, and bird eggs too.

A toucan's big bill is not useful at all for digging a nest hole. A breeding pair has to find a decayed hole in a rotting tree to use as a nest. Both parents take turns sitting on the eggs, but they are restless sitters. An hour at a time is enough for them.

Toucans are very playful. Three or four of them will often play catch with a piece of fruit. They like to wrestle too. They clasp their beaks together and push and pull until one is forced from its perch. Then another toucan steps in to wrestle with the victor.

Aracaris

FAMILY: Ramphastidae
COMMON EXAMPLE: Chestnut-eared aracari
GENUS AND SPECIES: *Pteroglossus castanotis*
SIZE: 14 1/2 inches (37 cm)

Like other toucans, the chestnut-eared aracari has a very large bill. It's not as big as a toco toucan's, but it is about a quarter of the length of its whole body. The bill has toothed edges, which help the aracari hold onto fruits, tender tree parts, insects, and the occasional small rodent.

Aracaris are social birds. They search for food together in small flocks, flying in single file through the woods and calling out, "Ku-sik, ku-sik, ku-sik!" At night, they roost in tree holes. Sometimes several of them will crowd into a single hole. Each one folds its head over its back, and then its tail over its head, so they can all fit in a small space.

Aracaris use old tree holes to lay their eggs and raise their young. They don't make nests inside. The young sit on old, regurgitated seed husks on the floor. The young that were born the year before usually help the parents raise the hatchlings. The whole group is kept busy bringing insects to the new hatchlings. As the young grow larger, the older birds bring them figs and other fruits to eat.

Every night, the adults crowd into the nest hole with their fledglings. It's cramped and stuffy, but it's also warm. About six weeks

after they hatch, the fledglings fly off on their own. But at night, the parents and their helpers lead them back to snuggle all together in the nest hole.

Honeyguides

FAMILY: Indicatoridae
COMMON EXAMPLE: Greater honeyguide
GENUS AND SPECIES: *Indicator indicator*
SIZE: 8 inches (20 cm)

Chattering loudly, a greater honeyguide leads a *honey badger* through the forest. It keeps stopping to make sure the honey badger is still following. Finally, it leads the honey badger to a bees' nest in a tree. The honey badger tears into the nest, gobbling up honey and bee *larvae*. The honeyguide waits nearby until the honey badger has eaten its fill. Finally, it's the honeyguide's turn. Now that the honey badger has opened the nest, the honeyguide dives in and starts eating the wax honeycombs and whatever bee larvae are left.

Honeyguides are the only birds that can digest wax. Scientists suspect that these birds have special bacteria in their guts that help them digest honeycombs. They also eat a lot of insects.

Honey badgers aren't the only animals that follow honeyguides to bees' nests. Baboons and mongooses do too, and so do humans. Many African tribes rely on honeyguides to help them find honey, which used to be their only source of sugar. They make the bees drowsy with wood smoke and open the hive with axes. Usually, the people leave some honeycomb for the honeyguides. They believe that if they don't, the birds will lead them into the den of a wild animal the next time they follow them.

Honeyguides don't make their own nests. They lay their eggs in the nests of other insect-eating birds. A newly hatched honeyguide has a sharp hook on the tip of its bill, which it uses to kill off the other young in the nest. When the parent birds bring insects, the young honeyguide gets them all to itself.

Barbets

FAMILY: Capitonidae
COMMON EXAMPLE: Yellow-fronted tinkerbird
GENUS AND SPECIES: *Pogoniulus chrysoconus*
SIZE: 4 1/2 inches (16.5 cm)

"Clink! Clink! Clink!" a tinkerbird calls as it flits about the trees. How did it get its name? People in Africa think that its call sounds like a pot-mender, or "tinker," mending his pots. Tinkerbirds, which are sometimes called "tinker barbets," repeat their call over and over and over all day long.

Tinkerbirds live in east-central Africa in open woodlands or in grassland with a few scattered trees. They feed mostly on berries or little insects.

Like other barbets, tinkerbirds have short, strong legs and spend most of their time climbing up tree trunks. Their short tails give them strong support as they climb. These birds are not very good fliers though. Their short, rounded wings are only good for flying short distances from tree to tree.

Tinkerbirds defend their territories fiercely, protecting both their food and their nest sites. They fly at intruders, calling loudly. Even larger birds, including woodpeckers, are scared of the little tinker-birds.

Pairs of yellow-fronted tinkerbirds stay together all year and have a long breeding season. A pair may raise three or four *broods* a year.

Tinkerbirds nest in tree holes. When the young are born, they are blind and naked and have leathery heel pads. They can use the tough pads to scrape out their nest holes to make them bigger.

Tinkerbirds have many broods a year because their hatchlings have a serious enemy. Honeyguides often lay their eggs in tinkerbird nests, and their hatchlings kill the young tinkerbirds.

Barbets

FAMILY: Capitonidae
COMMON EXAMPLE: Bearded barbet
GENUS AND SPECIES: *Lybius dubius*
SIZE: 10 inches (25 cm)

It's not hard to guess how the bearded barbet got its name. It has a big fringe of stiff whiskers all around its bill. Many other barbets also have "beards," but none are as whiskered as this one. The word "barbet" actually comes from the French word *barbu*, which means "bearded."

The bearded barbet has a big head and a large, stout, pointed bill. Notches on the bill help it grip its food. Together, the bill and the whiskers around it look like an adaptation for catching flying insects. Actually, bearded barbets feed mostly on fruit, especially wild figs. They are messy, clumsy feeders, and often drop the fruit they are trying to eat. Sometimes barbets will pluck an insect off a leaf or twig.

Groups of four or five bearded barbets travel together when hunting for food. At night, they roost together in a tree hole. All year long, they sing back and forth to each other, which helps them stake out their territories and stay together in a group.

At mating time, males start chasing after females. After they mate, they choose a dead tree, an old stump, or a termite mound in which they will dig out a nest hole. A barbet's stout beak doesn't look as though it would be much good for digging. However, it is

strong and pointed at the end, and it works well. The female lays only two eggs in the bottom of the hole. When the eggs hatch, both parents work hard to bring the young plenty of insects to eat. The young stay in the nest until they are well developed and able to fly.

Wrynecks

FAMILY: Picidae
EXAMPLE: Eurasian wryneck
GENUS AND SPECIES: *Jynx torquilla*
SIZE: 6 1/4 inches (16 cm)

"Kwee! Kwee! Kwee!" A male wryneck has found a hole in a tree that might make a good nest site. He calls to his mate, inviting her to look it over. She pokes her head in and then hops inside. She seems to like it because she starts throwing old nesting material out the door. She will lay her eight eggs on the bare floor.

For two weeks the adults take turns sitting on the eggs. For three weeks after they hatch, the parents tirelessly bring ants and ant *pupae* to the hungry hatchlings. Each baby eats about one thousand ants every day! Even after the fledglings leave the nest, their hardworking parents keep feeding and protecting them.

Wrynecks get their name from the way they guard their young in the nest. When an enemy comes near, they twist their necks and sway back and forth like a snake, hissing loudly. This usually scares small predators away. Maybe they think the wryneck *is* a snake!

Unlike many piciformes, especially woodpeckers and toucans, wrynecks are drab birds. Their brown-and-white patterned feathers help camouflage them among the bushes.

Wrynecks are becoming rare in Europe. Their nesting habitat and feeding grounds are being destroyed to make room for houses and

farmland, and the ants they need to eat are being killed by pesticides. In many places, such as England, wrynecks are in danger of disappearing entirely.

Woodpeckers

FAMILY: Picidae
COMMON EXAMPLE: Great spotted
  woodpecker
GENUS AND SPECIES: *Dendrocopos major*
SIZE: 9 inches (23 cm)

Rat-tat-tat-tat-tat! What is that racket? A male great spotted woodpecker has found a tree that will make a good nesting site. He drums loudly on the tree to attract a female. Soon the female shows up and begins chattering loudly at the male. All that noise drives him away so she can inspect the tree in peace. She likes it!

The birds start courting, chasing each other round and round the tree. Then they set to work digging a nest hole. Three weeks later, the nest is finally ready. Then the female lays a *clutch* of six creamy white eggs on the bare floor.

Male and female great spotted woodpeckers share the job of sitting on the eggs and bringing insects to the hatchlings. If a female gets killed before the young are ready to leave the nest, the male will raise the young alone. In between feedings, though, he will start his loud drumming again. Sometimes another female shows up and helps him finish the job of raising the young.

In the spring, you can see great spotted woodpeckers hopping up tree trunks searching for insects. They prop themselves against the trunks with their stiff tails and pry up pieces of bark with their

38

long, strong bill. They also chop deep into rotting wood, looking for grubs.

In the fall, these woodpeckers switch their diet to fruits, pinecone seeds, and nuts. They wedge large cones into clefts of trees. Then they rotate the cones in the clefts to pluck out the seeds on every side.

Woodpeckers

FAMILY: Picidae
COMMON EXAMPLE: European green
woodpecker
GENUS AND SPECIES: *Picus viridis*
SIZE: 12 1/2 inches (32 cm)

European green woodpeckers are large and brightly colored, but they can still be difficult to spot. Their green and yellow feathers help camouflage them among leaves or grass. They are also shy and wary. If you get too close, they will scuttle around to the other side of a tree to hide. In the spring, though, you may hear a male loudly calling out, "Klu-klu-klu-klu-klu-klu-klu!"

Green woodpeckers spend most of their time on the ground, sometimes quite far from the nearest tree. Their favorite food is ants. They peck funnel-shaped holes in ant nests and then spoon up the ants and larvae inside with their incredibly long, sticky tongues. A green woodpecker's tongue is four times as long as its bill!

These woodpeckers eat at least two thousand ants every day. They spend a long time at each anthill, trying to lick up every last ant. In the winter, they dig deep into the snow to find big nests of wood ants. But when the snow is too deep, many of the woodpeckers die. Even though they also feed on insects found under tree bark, they may not find enough insects to survive.

Like other woodpeckers, green woodpeckers hollow out holes in

trees to raise their young. They don't dig a new hole every year, though. They may use the same hole for ten years. After mating, a female lays one glossy white egg every morning until the clutch is complete. The parents take turns sitting on the eggs during the day, but at night the male takes on the job by himself. Once the young leave the nest, the parents split the brood. Each parent cares for half the fledglings.

Looking and Listening for Woodpeckers

A pair of binoculars will help you observe woodpeckers and other birds.

Many people enjoy bird watching, and woodpeckers are some of the easiest birds to hear and watch. Before you set off to find them, you should get a field guide to birds, a notebook to write down what you find, and a pair of binoculars. Most bird watchers prefer 10 x 40 binoculars, which make objects look ten times larger.

Spring is the best time to listen for woodpeckers. Males of many species drum loudly on trees, metal chimneys, or television antennas to attract their mates. Many also make very loud calls. In North America, listen for the loud "kik-kik-kikkik-kik-kik!" of a pileated woodpecker or the "wick-wick-wick-wick" of a flicker. In the west you might hear the raucous "ratchet, ratchet" of an acorn woodpecker. In Europe and Asia listen for the loud rattle of a great spotted woodpecker. Or, if you're lucky, you might hear the "klu-klu-klu-klu-klu-klu-klu" of the rare green woodpecker.

When you hear the drumming or calls, walk quietly toward the source. When you see the bird, keep your eyes on it and raise your binoculars. You can use your field guide to identify the bird. What does it look like? Where is it? Do you see more than one? What are they doing? Write down everything you notice.

Another good way to find woodpeckers is to look for their holes in trees. If you see fresh woodchips on the ground, you can

Look for adult woodpeckers bringing food back to their young.

bet that woodpeckers are nesting in a nearby tree. Watch to see if parents are flying back and forth, bringing food to their young. Do both the parents help? If you're lucky, you may see the newly fledged young flying out of the hole. Draw pictures and write down what you notice.

Many woodpeckers will also come to a *suet* holder hung outside in the winter. Downy and hairy woodpeckers will often come quite close to a house. Keep track of which woodpeckers come for the suet. How many different species can you count?

You can keep watching and listening for woodpeckers all year. You can become a woodpecker expert!

Words to Know

brood—a family of young

class—a group of creatures within a phylum that share certain characteristics

clutch—nestful of eggs

courting—performing actions and making sounds to attract a mate

divergent evolution—species in an order change over time to adapt to their specific habitats

family—a group of creatures within an order that share certain characteristics

fledgling—a young bird that has just grown feathers

genus (plural **genera**)—a group of creatures within a family that share certain characteristics

honey badger—a black-and-white carnivore, related to badgers, that feeds largely on honey

kingdom—one of the five divisions into which all living things are placed: the animal kingdom, the plant kingdom, the fungus kingdom, the moneran kingdom, and the protist kingdom

larva (plural **larvae**)—a young insect newly hatched from its egg

order—a group of creatures within a class that share certain characteristics

phylum (plural **phyla**)—a group of creatures within a kingdom that share certain characteristics

piciformes—the order of birds, including woodpeckers, toucans, barbets, and others that have zygodactyl feet and lay white eggs in holes

pupa (plural **pupae**)—the stage of an insect's life when it changes from a larva to an adult

salivary gland—an organ in an animal's mouth that produces saliva, or spit

species—a group of creatures within a genus that share certain characteristics. Members of a species can mate and produce young.

suet—hard beef or sheep fat that many birds enjoy eating

zygodactyl feet—feet of the piciformes, which have two toes pointing forward and two toes pointing backward

Learning More

Books

Dollar, Sam. *Toucans (Animals of the Rain Forest)*. Chatham, NJ: Raintree Steck-Vaughn, 2001.

Mania, Cathy and Robert C. Mania, Jr. *Woodpecker in the Backyard (Wildlife Conservation Society Books)*. Danbury, CT: Franklin Watts, 2000.

McDonald, Mary Ann. *Toucans (Naturebooks)*. New York: Child's World, 1998.

Peck, George K. *Woodpeckers*. New York: Smart Apple Media, 1998.

Peterson, Roger Tory. *Peterson's First Guide to the Birds*. Boston: Houghton Mifflin, 1997.

Winner, Cherie. *Woodpeckers (Carolrhoda Nature Watch Book)*. Minneapolis: Carolrhoda Books, 2000.

Video and CD-ROM

Audubon Society's VideoGuide to Birds of North America, vol. 3.

Web Sites

The Audubon Society
http://www.audubon.org
Watchlist feature that provides information about declining species, including many in the piciformes order.

Cornell Laboratory of Ornithology
http://www.ornith.cornell.edu
This site lets students participate in bird-watching projects. It also features a Bird of the Week, other bird projects, and information about how people can help protect birds.

Index

About the Author

Sara Swan Miller has worked with children all her life, first as a Montessori nursery-school teacher and later as an outdoor environmental educator at the Mohonk Preserve in New Paltz, NY. As director of the preserve school program, Miller has led hundreds of schoolchildren on field trips and taught them the importance of appreciating and respecting the natural world.

Miller has written a number of children's books, including *Three Stories You Can Read to Your Dog*; *Three Stories You Can Read to Your Cat*; *Three More Stories You Can Read to Your Dog*; *Three More Stories You Can Read to Your Cat*; *What's in the Woods? An Outdoor Activity Book*; *Oh, Cats of Camp Rabbitbone*; *Piggy in the Parlor and Other Tales*; *Better than TV*; and *Will You Sting Me? Will You Bite? The Truth About Some Scary-Looking Insects*. She has also written several books on farm animals for the Children's Press True Books series, a set of books on strange fishes, amphibians, reptiles, birds, and mammals for the Watts Library, and several other books in the Animals in Order series.